56,000
1,400
4,600